Why Israel Matters to You

Aryeh Spero

E**v**ergreen
PRESS
Mobile, Alabama

ISBN 978-1-58169-575-5
For Worldwide Distribution
Printed in the U.S.A.

Published by Evergreen Press in cooperation with
Team Focus
P.O. Box 91626 • Mobile, AL 36691
877-635-0010
E-mail: info@teamfocususa.org

Evergreen Press
P.O. Box 191540 • Mobile, AL 36619
800-367-8203
E-mail: info@evergreen777.com

Preface

There are moments in history when we are called upon to stand up on behalf of a great and transcendent cause. Now is such a moment. Today a propitious situation exists where what God wants and what represents our deepest beliefs are coalesced in one, unique issue. That issue and that cause are the survival and prospering of the State of Israel.

The battle is raging between those who wish to delegitimize and destroy Israel and those who see its establishment as being from the hand of God. Today's conflict is the final chapter in an age-old battle between the forces of light and the forces of darkness, the spirit of the Divine against the stench of idolatry, and freedom and dignity vs. tyranny and debasement of humankind. It is our battle and it is our once-in-a-lifetime opportunity to fight the good fight and stand against the impurity of the cynics, scoffers, and barbarians. We are lucky to be living in a time when our turn at the plate is crucial and all-defining.

The land of Israel and its connection to the Jewish people is singular. It is the only land that God assigned to a particular people as a Covenant between him and that people. Equally striking is how after almost 2,000 years of exile, a people returned to its land of origin and restored it to its intended promise. Zionism is an epoch phenomenon in the history of mankind. No one would have thought such a thing possible except the ancient prophets who had foretold it and the believers who, over centuries, kept faith. No one back then could have known the renascent Jewish state to be a future, unfolding reality except the author of history Himself, Almighty God.

Though four world empires conquered the land during the Jewish exiles, only the returned Jewish people were able to revive it and bring forth its fruit and celebration. For the land is their bride. God gave them Israel: Judea and Samaria. They toiled and sacrificed to resurrect it; they possessed it fairly and have died for it. It belongs to the Jewish people biblically, historically, legally, morally, and for reasons of personal sacrifice and devotion. They have conducted themselves nobly and fairly, far better than their never-ending critics and detractors.

Those in the Arab and Moslem world arrayed against Israel speak of instituting another Holocaust and gleefully celebrate the death of Jews in and out of Israel. For Islam, this is not a local battle over a few parcels of land but the desire and implementation of jihad against Israel and the West, against Jews and Christians— all considered infidels who must either convert, be destroyed, or live as third-class slaves under a ferocious and marching Islam. If the Israelis make a military blunder or allow the world to pressure them into "peaceful" surrender, they will be slaughtered.

What is at stake is not only Israel and western civilization, but the veracity of our Bible. Islam makes its claim against Israel by citing its Koran and rejecting the clear message and facts of our Bible. If Israel loses, they lose more than territory and freedom. Islam will declare its theology and view of how life should be lived as vindicated and supreme and, together with its new converts, be emboldened to attempt to subjugate the world.

It is only fitting that we proponents of the Judeo-Christian outlook and a strong America stand up for Israel now, since our beliefs and American foundations began back in the Holy Land. For the first time in 2,000 years, world events are finally bringing together serious biblical Christians and Torah Jews in a common cause that will determine our joint destiny.

Christian Zionists and other people of morality and sensible outlook display true character, courage, and principle when standing for Israel and against radical left dogma, Islamism, trendy political clichés, and the idolatries plaguing our society. We remain the genuine bearers of salt and light, of grit and earth from whence we were created. The call is now. It is the call of a lifetime, surfacing the best and strongest elements within our personhood and spirit.

This book is an attempt, in a fictional format, to explain what is really going on in the world today so that both young people and adults alike can stand firm on the correct side of history and support Israel.

Aryeh Spero, 2015

I

It was a nice sunny day in our town of Hartford City, Indiana. In fact, it was July, which is peak season here for playing baseball with the guys at the park just beyond the train tracks. It was a little after 10:00 a.m. as I crossed Main Street and made my way toward the railroad tracks so vital to the rhythm and lifeblood of our small town. Hartford City is close to many farms, and up until recently, also had numerous canning factories where vegetables, especially tomatoes, were processed and shipped across the country.

I heard the whistle of the daily 9:55 train sound off in the distance, as well as the rumble on the tracks as I headed to the park. This daily signal of movement through our town was comforting and reassuring, connecting us to destinations beyond from locations behind. We were still part of a dynamic American life, part of the action. Ebbets Park was beyond the tracks, and my friends with their bats and gloves were probably already in the field.

As I entered the park, I saw a middle aged man sitting on a green wooden bench that overlooks the field, reading a newspaper. I didn't recognize him and was certainly surprised at his tie and linen sport coat ensemble. All of us, especially at the park, wore just a t-shirt and jeans.

I glimpsed at the paper's headline, which read: "Israel Battling in Gaza to Stem Rocket Attacks." I knew it wasn't our local paper; this one was thicker and it had a print style and format that made it look, well, more like a big city paper. The headline above the fold seemed to convey something important, even urgent. I saw the date on the masthead: July 24, 2014.

When I reached the bench, the man introduced himself.

"Hello, young man, my name is Tom. I'm visiting my aunt, Susan McCray, and I just came in this morning on the 9:55 from Indianapolis. I'm expected for lunch so I'm a little early. Don't want to surprise my aunt by arriving before she's ready. I saw this bench and figured I'd wait here awhile, watch the game, and read my paper."

Tom was very pleasant, spoke with ease, yet with a type of determination. He seemed relaxed and secure with the surroundings.

"Welcome to Hartford City," I said as I stretched out my hand toward him. "My name is Lance and I'm a senior at Hartford High. I'm here to play some ball with my friends. Yes, I know Mrs. McCray. Her son, Matthew, went to our school." As I looked down at the headline, I remarked, "Looks like something big is happening over there, something important. Seems like a faraway place, yet somehow I feel it impacts me and that Israel is something I should get to know more about."

Tom nodded in agreement. "Tell you what, Lance. If you're interested in hearing more about this war and Israel, we can talk about it after your game. I'll give you my cell number, and you can call me if you'd like to come by later to talk. We could meet after lunch, either at my Aunt Susan's house on Chestnut or somewhere else."

"Great," I said, after he wrote down his number on a piece of paper and handed it to me. I liked Tom. I think it was no coincidence that I met a man who knows a lot about what's happening in Israel today while I had a big history project due soon on current events. I thought to myself, *This man knows some things I should get to know.*

"See you later, Tom," I said and shook his hand again before I ran over to join my friends in the baseball game.

Something in me said he was going to give me a vital understanding about today's world that would not only help me on my big project but also somehow change my future. I didn't quite know how, but I felt like I'd never be the same again.

I played a good game and got two singles, a walk, and a fly out with a run batted in. But we lost. An out-of-town friend of the other team blasted one over the wall in center, my position, in the eighth inning.

At 1:45, I headed toward Chestnut Street after I had called Tom and told him I was on my way. I stopped at Stein's Drugstore where I bought a Coke. I saw the local paper in the rack near the checkout counter, and while I waited in a long line, I picked it up and read the lead story about Israel. It turns out the country was defending herself against tunnels the Muslims had built from underneath Gaza to a kindergarten within Israeli territory. The Muslims had planned to secretly come out of the tunnels into the schoolyard and massacre all the Jewish kids. This was breaking news—no one seemed to have known about this plot or the tunnels until recently.

This news fascinated me so I bought the paper to finish reading the article on the bench outside Stein's. I found out that Hamas, the governing body of Gaza, used money the world had sent for building schools and hospitals and, instead, had built wide concrete underground tunnels to kill Israelis. The concrete that was brought into the country for hospital construction was a ruse. Israel had suspected something like this, but when in the previous summer they tried to block ships entering Gaza with the concrete, the U.N. and most of Europe accused the Israelis of blocking humanitarian supplies.

The Gaza strip had been under Israeli control ever since they had captured it during the Six Day War way back in 1967 after they had been attacked by the Arab armies. The U.N. and others had demanded that Israel forfeit this strategic defense barrier for the sake of peace. It seemed that Israel was constantly giving up territory and releasing prisoners who had killed Israelis...all for the sake of peace. And this was going on for more than 40 years.

The paper had a side article that explained more about Gaza. Fascinated, I read on. Instead of peace, all the Israelis got from Gaza were rockets aimed at her cities, children, farms, and schools along with tunnels designed for their slaughter. Instead of the Muslims building a productive society for themselves, something they claimed to the world they desired, they spent their energies on the destruction of Israel, as well as routing money from world agencies into the pockets of its two main factions, Hamas and Fatah. It turns out that Gaza became a terrorist state, a beachhead against Israel and a training ground for worldwide terrorism against the West, and even America.

Folding up the paper, I got up and hurried the few streets to the McCray house. Its front porch was filled with a two-seat glider, a couple of wicker chairs stuffed with cushions, and planters filled with petunias and carnations. Four steps up the porch and I was in front of a brown wooden door with an oval shaped window covered on the inside with white embroidered lace. I rang the bell and Mrs. McCray answered, Tom standing behind her with his linen coat off but his striped tie still on.

"Come in," she welcomed me.

I vaguely recognized Mrs. McCray from church. I had also seen her at school picnics back in the days when she served on the PTA.

"I met Lance this morning at the park," Tom said, turning to the woman, "and we're going to talk about Israel."

"How wonderful!" Mrs. McCray beamed. "You know, Lance, twenty years ago when I was much younger, a group of us from church took a trip to Israel. It was the most exhilarating and deeply satisfying trip I've ever taken. It remains in my mind always. Oh the history and beauty of the land! I was overwhelmed by how much sweat and sacrifice the Jewish people have made for the rebirth of the State of Israel and how beautiful they have made its countryside with lush orchards, olive groves, wheat fields, and dairy farms. They brought water to parched lands and removed dangerous water from malaria infested ponds. Just as the biblical prophets predicted, they have truly made the desert bloom."

As we made ourselves comfortable in the tidy living room, Mrs. McCray continued: "I was also impressed by the modern hospitals and cities they have built that are thriving. The children sing and the schools ring out with learning. The land is their destiny. It is obvious!

"On our trip, we walked the pathways where Abraham, Isaac, and Jacob had walked, and traveled the entirety of Israel, from the Jordan River to the Mediterranean. We viewed everything from the mountain top where Moses had gazed forth to the Jewish holy city of Hebron, where the first family of Judaism is buried in the Cave of the Machpellah. Did you know that Abraham first purchased it after the death of his beloved wife, Sarah? Buried there are Abraham and Sarah, Isaac and Rebecca, Jacob and Leah."

Mrs. McCray was on a roll now. You could tell she had really enjoyed her trip to Israel and had done a lot of reading about it. I figured all this information would really give me some good background to my current events history report so I listened carefully.

After offering us some lemonade, which we both said we'd have later, the older woman continued with her story: "We saw where King David had built Jerusalem in Israel, the Jewish people's eternal capital that was ordained and blessed by God Himself. We sat where Abraham, at Bethel and later Mamre, made a covenant with God and was repeatedly promised this land by him as an inheritance to his children, to Isaac and his son, Jacob, and eventually the twelve tribes of Israel. We saw where Isaac was almost sacrificed atop Mount Moriah, the location of the future Jewish Temple, the elevated spot where King Solomon actually built the Temple, and where Ezra rebuilt it, and Herod beautified it."

Mrs. McCray stopped for a minute, and her face suddenly looked sad. "Years ago," she began again, "when the Arabs conquered Jerusalem from its rightful Jewish owners, they did not allow the Jews to pray on the Mount or in other parts of Jerusalem, and they treated the Christian population as *dhimmis*, the Islamic term for second class. The Muslims controlled the holy sites with unfairness and by humiliating non-Muslims. They even took the precious stones of synagogues and tombstones of the Jewish dead and defiled them by using them as places for urination. They are doing the same today with churches they are conquering throughout Asia, the Middle East, and Africa, as well as the sacred places of Hindus, Buddhists, Yazidis, and Zoroasters. In the formerly Christian cities of Bethlehem and Nazareth, the Muslims in the neighborhood intimidate the Christians and decide what type of access and freedom they are allowed."

Brightening up a bit, she added, "But ever since the Jewish people recaptured Jerusalem, their holy city, after being attacked by five Arab armies, Jerusalem has been open for all to pray as equals. For example, we walked the Via Dolorosa where Jesus on route to Calvary carried the Cross. We saw Bethlehem, where Jacob's wife, Rachel, died and where Jesus was born; and we passed through Nazareth where Jesus worked as a Jewish carpenter. We were frankly disappointed that fewer and fewer Christians now inhabit these holy cities. They've been purged by the Muslims who want these cities bled of their Jewish and Christian history in order to reconfigure them as Muslim cities, pretending they always were Muslim, though we know they were originally Jewish and Christian."

A look of anger flashed over her face. "They want to rewrite history to claim they always possessed these places, that every place they now inhabit was always Muslim territory, and that most important things were accomplished by Muslims. But Jews know their history, and they will not let themselves be robbed of their well-earned heritage by allowing the facts to be changed!"

I looked over at Tom and he nodded in understanding. After a long sigh, Mrs. McCray glanced at us and smiled. "Oh yes, and we also saw the Garden of Gethsemane and the Church of the Holy Sepulcher. Later we went to the beautiful Sea of Galilee where Jesus gave his Sermon on the Mount, a compilation of wonderful and sacred ideas and yearnings from the Torah, Psalms, Talmud, and Gospels. Jesus, you know, was Jewish. The stunning Sea of Galilee, deep and shaped like a harp, is where Jesus performed many miracles and impressed his followers and later mankind."

I had never thought of Jesus as Jewish; but, of course, he must have been, seeing that his lineage is traced back to David from the tribe of Judah, the son of Jacob the Hebrew, also known as Israel.

"Oh what a trip it was. I'd take one trip to Israel, the biblical Holy Land, over ten trips to Las Vegas, any day. It changed my life. All this was made possible since the reestablishment of Israel by those rugged and idealistic 20th century Jewish pioneers, who sacrificed and died for the land. They are agents of God Himself, where, as in the days of old, God has stretched forth his hand to the covenanted land. It is another entering into the Promised Land, but now, I believe, the final one. The first was after the bondage of Egypt; the second, after the exile to Babylon; and this one, after the Holocaust and Soviet Gulag. All three entries were foretold in the Torah and by the prophets."

She shook her head. "Well, enough from me. I'm going to get the lemonade and some sugar cookies from Jensen's Bakery. Here, why don't you and my nephew talk and enjoy yourself this fine Indiana afternoon. Tom will be here only a few days. He has to get back to Canton. He's first going to Chicago and then he'll be taking the train eastward. See you later, Lance. It's a pleasure having you here in our home."

II

Taking our lemonade and cookies with us, we went out onto the porch and Tom motioned for me to take one of the wicker chairs, the one closer to the door. I sat down, feeling unusually comfortable with this guy I had just met this morning. He seemed very honest and straightforward. His tone and mannerisms were pleasant, very Midwest.

"Lance," he began, "my interest in Israel began during my time in the Navy where we would often disembark at the Haifa port after weeks of military exercises in the Mediterranean. It hadn't occurred to me until sometime later that Elijah the Prophet spent his time looking out at the very Mediterranean Sea our ship cruised and that he spent the most daring episode of his life right there by Haifa on Mt. Carmel.

"It was there that Elijah challenged the false prophets of Baal to prove that their gods were the true God. Fire came down from heaven and devoured Elijah's sacrifice but failed to do so for their sacrifice. While the false prophets wailed to their gods to demonstrate their power, the nation witnessed the truth of Adonai. The false prophets ran from the wrath of the people who now realized how deceitful the false prophets had been.

"I often wonder whether we'll ever publicly demonstrate our beliefs and stand up against cultural false prophets in our midst, if we too could awaken the people and take our country back from those determined to radically transform it. During the three years we docked in and out of Haifa, I grew to marvel at the resiliency of the people against enemies sworn from day one to destroy them. I also appreciated the steady and creative energy they put into building their country for themselves and their posterity. But, most of all, I was enamored by the land."

"What's so special about the land?" I had been itching to ask that question during Mrs. McCray's description of it.

"Think of it, Lance. What other land is so significant that it was chosen by God as a gift and inheritance to a particular people? It's a land that God calls his own. God, of course, made all the lands of the world, but with Israel he had a special relationship and bond. He, personally, would determine its rainfall, its weather, and its blessings.

"And to it, he attached a particular people, the Hebrews, the Jewish people, specifically, the seed of Isaac: "For in Isaac I shall call your seed." He reiterated to Isaac and later Jacob, to Moses and later Joshua, to Samuel and later Hezekiah that this land, God's land, was to be the inheritance of the Jewish people.

"Now, don't get me wrong. I love America and that's where I want to live…and die. I love our people, our Constitution and Declaration, our Judeo-Christian ethos, the magnanimity, generosity, and idealism of the majority of our citizens, the great men that founded it, our values, history, rugged individualism, music, holidays, good cheer, and sense of fair play…and its power. But the special land covenant of Israel is singular because it is the one between God and the family of Israel and those who cherish and protect it. I support Israel because I believe in God and his Word. I want to be on God's team."

"So, I imagine," I responded, "that all Christians support Israel, seeing how its rebirth as a State has been foretold by the prophets and that its promise to the Jewish nation is emphasized in the Bible so many times."

Tom took a moment to reply and then said: "Well, yes, it should be that way, but it hasn't always worked out that way. You see, many of the early Christians believed that Christianity had come to replace Judaism, and Christian people had come to replace Jewish people as those covenanted with God. Some even went so far as to basically nullify the Old Testament as irrelevant and even primitive. They maintained that the passages from Genesis to Deuteronomy, from Joshua to Jeremiah, from Psalms to Zachariah were of little significance when it came to the relationship between God and the Jewish people, as well as his promise to them regarding the land."

Now that was a surprise to me, but I had never really read much about the subject. I really was receiving important information that I would need for my report.

"For centuries," Tom went on, "nearly two thousand years in fact, the Catholic Church felt it had replaced the Jewish people and, worse, that the Jewish people had been formally rejected by God. They, therefore, would not support the rebuilding of the land or the Jewish desire and prayers to be reunited to the land, restored to their ancient Commonwealth.

"Even today, and especially in Europe, much of the Catholic hierarchy simply cannot come to terms with a Jewish State, since it forces them to reconsider centuries of theology casting the Jews and their land from the annals of biblical veracity. And sometimes, as a way to justify what many call its 'replacement theology' and dilemma regarding Israel, it will condemn Israel for doing this or that small thing, as a way of saying that she has not earned the right to continue existing.

"Sometimes, the Church and others will raise the bar of required conduct so high that, short of perfection, the Jewish State is not granted any type of embrace. If other nations and people were required to be almost perfect, or beyond perfect, as a condition for existence, I dare say no nation could be given a stamp of approval."

When Tom paused to eat a cookie and sip some lemonade, I thought for a minute and then asked him, "What about here in America?"

"It's better here," he answered. "First off, many Catholics are friendly with Jewish people and understand the great attachment and importance of Israel to their Jewish friends. European Catholics and Jews never had a warm and friendly relationship during centuries of Jews living in Europe. Besides, many American Catholics admire Israel for being a democracy, a land of liberty and innovation, and one that shares our American values. They realize that the Arab and Muslim states, hell-bent on destroying Israel and the Jewish people, live by a set of rules, beliefs, and a code almost polar opposite ours.

"Many American Catholics remain horrified by the Holocaust, when the Nazis deliberately killed over six million Jews in Europe during World War II, and understand the need for a Jewish State so that Jews will not find themselves again in a similar circumstance somewhere else in the world. They know that, just as with all other nations, the Jewish people need an army and police to protect them and that many countries are filled with those who would love to murder their Jewish population.

"Part of the test and dilemma of being a people of God is that people want to eradicate you, as a way of saying, 'See, you're not invincible. Where's your God? We are stronger than God.' Today, Christians are being similarly attacked by Islamists and rabid secularists."

"What about Europe? How do they feel since they were closer to the Holocaust than we were?" I asked him.

"Europeans, in general, do not seem to share the same noble feelings as do Americans. Centuries of Jew hatred have left them somewhat unfazed by the Holocaust and, indeed, one of the ways of relieving themselves of any Holocaust guilt and complicity perpetrated in their midst is to condemn Israel or the Jewish people for almost everything under the sun, as a way, almost, of saying: 'See, they deserved it! We didn't do such a bad thing after all.'

"In fact, in Europe today, anti-Semitism—a fancy phrase for Jew hatred—is on the rise and synagogues are once again being burned, Jewish shops and schools are being firebombed, and Jewish rabbis and school children are being beaten up mostly by

Muslim immigrants within Europe, but with the quiet acquiescence of European bystanders. Jews are flocking out of France, Belgium, and even Sweden each week in response to this wave of brutality. Where are they going? Bingo! Israel—their place of refuge. It appears to be part of God's plan: all part of the foretold 'Ingathering of the Exiled.'"

That was another big surprise for me. I guess I really need to keep up better with current events. I had no idea that sort of thing was going on today in the 21st century.

"Nor do many Europeans share American values—they are deeply socialist and cynical. They are not moved by Israeli innovation, its sense of liberty, its fight against evil, nor its American values. In fact, to the degree that Israel becomes more and more free-market oriented, fights evil, and reflects historic American values do Europeans become distanced from it."

I interrupted Tom: "You mean after all we did for Europe in World War II, all the American lives that were lost to save their countries from destruction, they don't like us?"

"No, they don't, Lance. And Israel was founded with an attitude and ways similar to America. Both countries had a specific platform, a sense of divine destiny, with pioneers sacrificing and risking all to build a land between the waterways, the Jordan to the Mediterranean, the Atlantic to the Pacific. Both lands were built according to biblical philosophic principles. Both are countries with specific national identities, something socialist and Universalist ideologues disdain."

"Getting back to what you said about the church, what about the Protestants?" I asked.

"Well, that's a completely different story," he answered with a warm smile on his face. "Israel has no greater friends in the world today than the American Evangelical community. The reason for that is threefold. One is their belief in Scripture. Two, their conservative beliefs. And three, their belief in liberty and fighting against evil, be it communism or Islamism.

"Years ago, Israel was our main ally in the Middle East fighting the communists and Soviet Union. The Arab countries were all clients of the Soviets. And today, Israel is in the fore-front in fighting Islamism. Islamists want to first destroy Israel, which they call the Little Satan, and then America, which they call the Big Satan. After two thousand years of separation be-tween the Christian and Jewish communities, many are joining together in a fight for common values and a battle for physical survival."

Tom leaned forward as if to emphasize what he was going to say next. "And that's another reason why I support Israel. It's on the front lines in the fight against terrorism. They're up against Hamas and Hezbollah and Fatah. These are all terrorist groups, not much different than the Muslim Brotherhood, Al-Qaida, and the Taliban. They all want Islamic control, a caliphate, a world under Islamic law.

"In every region, these groups try to make it appear as if they are engaged in only a local skirmish, demanding only this small amount of territory today. But when they get one parcel of land, they claim another, each time justifying their new claim under some new concocted grievance. They've taken over the entire Middle East and other countries street by street, neigh-borhood by neighborhood, city by city, and country by country."

Tom took a sugar cookie and offered me one. It was my second of the afternoon. "How about we get up for a while and walk down the street so we can get some blood flowing back to the muscles?"

"Good idea, I'm all for that," I answered. We walked down the steps of the porch and over the slate stoneway leading from the porch to the sidewalk.

As we turned left onto the sidewalk leading toward town, Tom took up our conversation. "Let me share some more his-tory with you," he said. "You know, when I was younger, Lebanon was a majority Christian country. Now it's run by

Hezbollah, an Islamic terrorist group. Ancient Egypt was not Islamic, rather it was the center of Greek learning and culture on the southern Mediterranean. Now it's Islamic. Most of what is today called Syria and Iraq were biblical Christian communities. Iran was a Persian country. They are now all Islamic, with only traces of their former Christian or Persian way of life. It was terrorism then, and it's terrorism now.

"Today's stakes are even higher, for the appetite of the Islamic terrorists is greater and at their disposal are potential weapons of mass destruction. I support Israel because it is the last buffer between the Middle East and Europe and the Middle East and America. You know, Israel is like the canary in the mine."

"What do you mean by that?" I asked, not sure what birds had to do with the subject.

"You know when miners go down the shaft into the mine they bring with them a canary, and that's because a canary is very sensitive to gases and is the first of creatures to die from poison gas. If the mine has these gases build up, the canary dies, which immediately alerts the miners to start protecting themselves. The same is true with the Jewish people. They're like canaries. Hitler, for example, went after them first. The world should have known that once the Jews were killed, others would be next. And so it was. Hitler started with the Jews but then went after mankind.

"The Muslims have declared war on Israel. They want Israel and the Jews gone. It also means, after the Jews, the world is next. In fact, we are already seeing this with entire Christian communities—the Coptics, Maronites, Black Christians, Nigerians, and others—being killed by Islamists. Millions have been slaughtered!"

Now that boggled my mind. Millions? Now? I shook my head as we turned the corner.

Tom's voice rose a little. I suspected he was getting a little worked up by talking about it. "I support Israel because it is fighting evil. Our Bible commands us to fight evil. That's one of our main obligations here on earth. And yes, pray for the peace and security of Jerusalem. Pray for her strength. Support her. And do you know what? Our very lives depend upon it!"

We walked along in silence for a bit while I thought about the implications of what he had just said.

"The main thing to keep in mind about conservative Evangelicals," Tom continued, "is that they take Scripture at its word and don't look at Scripture as merely symbolic or as a metaphor or as something to be arbitrarily changed. When God says the land belongs to the Jewish people, they believe it. Unlike some of today's so-called mainline Protestants who believe in Replacement Theology, most Evangelicals believe that the Jewish covenant remains, which in no way dilutes from the new covenant between New Testament believers and the Lord.

"Furthermore, a high proportion of Evangelical believers and preachers remind us of what God told Abraham during their first encounter in the Land of Canaan, the Land of Israel: 'I shall bless those that bless you and punish those that curse you.'

"Some examples? Well, the Egyptian army and Pharaoh were destroyed in the Red Sea. Some empires out to destroy ancient Israel or the Jewish people had their fall not immediately but soon thereafter—Babylon was brought down by Persia within fifty years of destroying Solomon's Temple; Haman plotted against the Jews and eventually hung from the very gallows he had prepared for Mordechai, the Jewish sage; Rome eventually fell to the barbarians; Spain, who administered the Inquisition and kicked out its Jews, eventually fell and is now a has-been, decaying place; not to mention Germany, which fell and was divided for 40 years, and the former Soviet Union. Even ancient Assyria, which captured and dispersed the Ten Tribes, is now having its remnant monuments destroyed.

"Yet, Israel has been reborn, surpassing Babylon (Iraq), Egypt, Spain, and Russia in freedom, technology, progress, and love of its citizens for its country. America, up until the Obama regime, has been a great friend of Israel. Harry Truman recognized the new country on that crucial day in 1948 when it announced its statehood, though one wonders if Barack Obama would be among those recognizing the State of Israel if it were today first announcing its statehood."

Wow, I was learning a history I had not really known before. I hadn't realized how long the Jews had been around and how they were at the intersection of every space and moment throughout history.

III

We returned to the porch. "Lance, how about some more lemonade?" Gratefully I held up my glass. We had been walking for almost an hour and by the time we got back, the ice in the pitcher had melted. After pouring me some, Tom took a sip of his, quickly finishing the remainder. He loosened his tie, opened up his top shirt button, and breathed deeply in from a soft breeze wafting across the porch. He looked around, appreciating the fine lawn and flower beds bordering the porch.

We sat back down and sighed in unison. He continued: "You know, the Pilgrims and Puritans who founded this country in the mold of a new Promised Land, did so with the signet of biblical impression, naming America's new towns, for example, Bethel, Kidron, Salem, New Canaan, Efrat, Bethlehem, Hebron, and Shiloh. They depicted on the coinage the Jews crossing the parted Red Sea, with a motto 'Renunciation of Tyrants is Service to God.' The emotional connection between Israel and America is as old as Plymouth Rock itself.

"Generally, conservative Protestant Christians who identify with America's original founding, wishing to preserve it and seeing it as an inspiration, look enthusiastically upon the Jewish state and want to be part of its growth and destiny. In fact, with the recent phenomenon of American Catholics embracing the Old Testament, support for Israel among conservative Catholics has grown too. Few people know that in mid nineteenth century America, there were many Old Testament, Scripture-oriented theologians, preachers, and activists who called for the ingathering of the oppressed Jewish exiles to a re-born Jewish state in what was then called Palestine. Early in the 20th century, Presidents Wilson and Harding asked the League of Nations to help establish a Jewish state in the area of present day Israel, from the Mediterranean to the Jordan River, actually about 100 miles beyond the Jordan eastward."

"What about Islam?" I asked Tom.

"Islam has not, nor will it probably ever, accept a Jewish state, nor a Jewish presence, except as dhimmis, second class citizens subservient to Islam, paying special taxes to it, and restricting its religious worship, industry, and learning to the limits Islam will impose on it. Jews were living in the Israel region 2,200 years before Islam was founded and hundreds of years before Arabs began moving in. Way before the establishment of the modern State of Israel, Muslims, in what the Romans labeled Palestine, butchered Jews in Hebron, Safed, and even Jerusalem. They seem to do that a lot—too much, too often, and in too many places."

"I can see that. But how did the Muslims ever get involved in Israel in the first place?" I asked.

"After the fall of Rome, the Muslims conquered Jerusalem and purposely built a mosque atop the Temple Mount so as to declare their ownership of that space. Islam has never approved of Jewish life in the Holy Land. Funny that Islam should try to lay claim to Jerusalem when Jerusalem is never mentioned even once in the Koran while being mentioned over 700 times in the Jewish Torah, the Old Testament. It was a Holy Land for Jews and, later, Christians. Never Islam. But once Islam captures a parcel of land, it declares its ownership over it in perpetuity."

"You're kidding. But that's ridiculous!" I replied.

"Yes, it has done so with all the territories it has conquered. For example, Islam conquered Constantinople, the seat of Byzantine Christianity, and converted the famed and beautiful St. Sophia Church into a mosque. It became their 'mosque of triumph,' a symbol of their having conquered Christianity.

"Conquering others and co-opting their holy places are primary goals of Islam. They have gone from a tribe in one small town, Medina, in Arabia, to now controlling 1/3 of the world's territory and population, areas that were once Christian, Persian, Chaldean, Hindu, Asian, and African, making the land and its people Islamic.

"Such is the power of the sword, the power of an army invading those not anticipating invasion, the power of a population inside a country stealthily plotting an uprising over an unsuspecting citizenry that had previously invited them in. Even Malaysia and Indonesia, countries that are not Arabic but Asian, were conquered and are now Islamic; so too are the Balkans.

"Using history as our guide, Islam will never accept the Jewish state; to the contrary, their goal is to destroy it and take it for themselves. Every overture Israel has made for peace—and there have been dozens—is in the end rebuffed by some excuse or another. Israel has no luxury on its side. Israel has won its wars of defense. If it loses even one to the Arabs, it will be wiped away, if not at once, then assuredly piecemeal. The Arab/Muslims simply do not recognize the existence of Israel nor recognize it as a Jewish state.

"While Islam is a political ideology, it is also a religion, though imbibing values very different than our Judeo-Christian ethos. When they mention peace, justice, or mercy in the Koran, it is not peace or justice for Jews and Christians, the 'infidels,' but peace and justice for Muslims, within the Muslim community."

"That's a selfish attitude, for sure! Definitely not noble!" I said.

"At this very moment," Tom continued, "Islamic religious organizations are digging below the Temple Mount where they assemble the remains of vessels and artifacts of ancient Jewish/Judean character and destroy them, pulverizing them into garbage in order to bury the history of Jerusalem's Jewish presence in preparation of declaring a city 'always' Islamic.

When the Israelis try to stop this carnage and trashing of history, they are accused of 'violating the rights of Muslims at their holy places.'

"Many in the Islamic world claim that as descendants of Abraham through Ishmael, they are entitled to the land. But, as shown throughout the Bible, whereas Ishmael was a son of Abraham, Isaac constitutes Abraham's lineage and is heir to the land and the promises made to Abraham. Isaac is the inheritor, the spiritual heir apparent. Isaac was from Abraham's wife, Sarah, his family; whereas Ishmael was born from Hagar, a concubine. This is clear in all readings of the Bible. Abraham blessed Isaac, not Ishmael. Ishmael was banished due to 'his affliction of Isaac and Hagar's taunting of Sarah.'

"In fact, of Ishmael the Bible writes: 'And he shall be wild; his hands into everyone else and everyone into him, and he shall dwell in-your-face.' Ishmael is not buried in the family plot at the Cave of Machpellah in Hebron. But the Koran disregards much of this, since it does not recognize the Bible in its integrity. The New Testament is born of the Old, an offshoot whose nourishment derives from the Old. Therein is its legitimacy. That is why we speak of a Judeo-Christian ethos. Jesus was Jewish, the prophecies are his cradle. Islam's Koran, on the other hand, does not feel bound by the Bible; it does not revere it except to use it selectively to create its pre-disposed Islamic narrative. Mohammed was not Jewish.

"Mohammed killed the Jews of Medina, who mistakenly trusted him and invited him to live among them. He and his men beheaded 700 Jewish men, women, and children. He repaid their friendship and trust with scorn, anger, and death. He did it through what is called and praised in Arabic as *tequiah*, lying and fooling the enemy, in pursuit of Islamic dominance, by saying those things your host wants to hear. It becomes a lullaby of death.

"For hundreds of years thereafter, except for a narrow period in Spain, Jews suffered tremendously in Arab lands: pogroms, ghettos, beatings, murders, yellow bands, blood libels, and rapes. Then there's the alliance between the Islamic Grand Mufti and Hitler, and the expulsion of almost 900,000 Jews from their homes in Arabic lands after the establishment in 1948 of the State of Israel."

I had a feeling this morning when I first talked to Tom that my eyes would be opened to things I had not really known before. Our conversation became personal, something connected to my Christianity and my Americanism, and began alerting me to the threats to our civilization from the forces wanting to destroy Israel and my home, America.

IV

Time was flying by. This encounter seemed to me to be one of those chance events one has that ends up being life-changing. Sometimes people come into our lives and then out, in a one-time encounter, and the effect is greater than routine meetings we have with people dozens of times. We stood up and walked toward Main Street.

"Tom," I asked, "what do you do for a living?"

"I'm a manager of a specialty steel company that makes pipes and rods for the oil-gas drilling business," he answered. He told me he was forty years old and had been married but lost his wife to an illness. He stared off into the distance for awhile and didn't add anything more. I didn't want to ask him any more questions.

Suddenly he said: "My wife's name was Barbara. I met her in Israel at the American consulate in Tel Aviv. She was from Pittsburgh. She was a Steelers fan and I rooted for the Browns. That's what started it all. I was at the Consulate to arrange something, and the sports page from the *International Herald Tribune* was open on her desk to an article about the upcoming, eagerly awaited annual game between Cleveland and Pittsburgh. Well, I mentioned something about the Browns from back home and before you know it, we were off to the races."

I laughed, remembering some disagreements about sports teams I'd had with some of my friends.

"I remember Barbara telling me that first time about something interesting Mark Twain had written about the Holy Land, in those days called Palestine. You've read Mark Twain, I suppose?"

"Oh yeah," I answered, "Tom Sawyer, Huckleberry Finn."

"Mark Twain had traveled there in the late 1800s," Tom continued, "before the vast arrival of Jews to Israel in the early 1900s. There had always been a Jewish presence in Palestine, even after the destruction of the Temple and the subsequent exile in the Third Century AD. In fact, the Jewish community in Jerusalem, though small, was the largest of any single group—more than the nomads or Arabs or the Christians during the Crusades. Yet the Jews were not in control. They had not had an official state there since the Roman takeover, around the time of Jesus. Rome, Arabs, the Ottomans...they all had ruled there at one time or another.

"The last empire to rule over the land was the British, and they called the Jewish population "Palestinians." If the Jews had not decided to name their state Israel, they would still be called Palestinians. In fact, what we now call the *Jerusalem Post* newspaper, a Jewish newspaper, was then called the *Palestinian Post*. Anyway, getting back to Twain. After his visit, he said, 'the land was full of thistles and thorns, barren, parched, bereft of trees, full of stones, not fit for habitation, and there were no thriving cities.'"

"How could that be? How could a land remain barren and unfit for life for 2,000 years when great empires had been in control of it?" I asked.

Tom smiled and answered: "How could it be that only after the Jews returned en masse and began a state did the desert bloom, the land flourish, the trees grow tall, the cities rise, and the air emit the aroma of a vibrant civilization? Here, Lance, my friend, is the ultimate answer and reality. Only the Jewish people can make this land thrive. No one else. That's the underlying theme of this covenant between this specific land and its specific, rightful landlord. Not the Romans, not the Arabs, nor the Ottomans could do it. It is a land whose bounty depends on a specific planter, like a race horse tied to its jockey.

"You see, it takes a people who loved this land with a unique and special love to tend it, sacrifice for it, nurture it, and speak to it in the way that the land hears and obeys. To the Romans, the Arabs, the Ottomans, the British, it was just another piece of land. To the Jews, however, it is their bride. Only the Jews had prayed for this land, three times a day for more than 2,000 years, even while they were away from it. Their heart is tied to the land, and the land's soul and spirit is in them."

Now that made sense to me. If something is truly yours, you will take much better care of it than if it were a neighbor's.

Tom continued: "There is in Israel what is called the Green Line. It's the agricultural line dividing the Jewish side from where the Arabs live. The Israeli side is green and fertile, robust and fresh. The Arab side is parched, desolate, boring, and untended—same weather, same conditions, same rocks. But the keepers of one side have love for the land, while the Arab rulers have no special emotion attached to it, except that they don't want Israel to have it.

"Those historic Jewish returnees to Israel had no special advantage. Their tools were their hands; they had crude and old farm implements. They came back to the land with nothing except a full determination to revive it. They didn't even have homes. But they belonged to the land and the land belonged to them.

"Never in the history of mankind has a nation been exiled from its land to miraculously return after 1,800 years. They retained its language, Hebrew, remembered its hills and valleys, and kept its memory and immediacy alive by harboring it in their collective heart. It's a miracle, a divine fulfillment. It is Providence similar to the Providence of Philadelphia in 1776. God guides the land of Israel when it's in the hands of the Jewish people.

"The single greatest national event and epoch of the twentieth century is called Zionism, the movement to resurrect a land and make it live and thrive once again. It is an inspiring saga that I want to be part of. I identify with it because I cherish great sacrifice and inspired hard work, and because I feel uplifted linking myself to God's active hand in history. God, so to speak, has kept his word."

Wow! I was moved by what Tom had just said. Yes, there truly is something above the ordinary about the epoch rebuilding and resettlement of the land of Israel by the Jewish people.

We were in front of Jensen's Bakery, which is between Logan's Hardware Store and Parcell's Shoe Store. Tom took out his cell phone.

"See this?" he asked. "Did you know that the voice mail, text messaging, and most of the digital mechanisms, as well as the firewall to protect your information from hackers were all invented and developed in Israel?" I had not. "Next to the U.S., Israel is the country coming up with the most technological products in the world today. And they're products that make life better for each of us.

"That's quite an accomplishment when you realize that they've been invaded by Arabic and Islamic armies seven times in 60 years, and that almost daily, Islamic groups are firing rockets into Israel and sending suicide bombers to kill civilians. And get this—almost all of its young people have to defer their college education until they've served and finished their army stint to protect the country. It's a true civilian army, just as in the time of the Bible and as it was during the American Revolution."

That amazed me. If I were in Israel, I'd spend the next couple years of my life in the army. And that was normal for their young people!

He put his cell phone back in his pocket. "All of the major technology companies, be they Intel, Microsoft, or Motorola, have primary research facilities there—not in England or Italy, not in Saudi Arabia or Malaysia. It is in Israel where the major breakthrough is taking place to transform sea water into drink-able and irrigational water—de-salinization. Drip-water irrigation was invented in Israel for climates around the world lacking enough rain water such as our American Southwest. More miracle drugs for the heart and head, and to fight cancer, improve eyes, and for safe surgery are invented here than any other place, except the U.S.

"Israel, next to America, is the first one on the scene when natural calamities take place in the world, such as hurricanes, earthquakes, tsunamis. The Arab countries are awash in money from their oil wells, yet one hardly ever sees them aiding other countries. Israel was there in Haiti and in Africa with doctors and emergency medical units before countries much wealthier than her.

"That's another reason I support Israel. It is a paradigm for the productive side of life, a generous society that reaches out, takes on responsibility, and works daily to achieve and accomplish. It's inspiring."

"It's certainly inspiring to me," I said. "With so much good coming from such a small country, it's sad that they are so hated."

"I want to back those societies like Israel," Tom went on, "that believe in working and doing, instead of those endlessly agitating, complaining, demanding handouts, or using their energy and brainpower to destroy. I'm alarmed by societies and cultures that often threaten and intimidate other countries into submission and force them to live by inhumane laws dating back to barbaric times. I believe in the work ethic, not one that says 'I'm owed a handout.' I believe God sent us here to create, not destroy. I believe in live and let live, not the imposition of communism or Sharia law. Israel represents civilized, forward-looking society."

I agreed wholeheartedly. So, Israel must certainly have a lot of support in the world, I thought. But I remembered watching the news and seeing delegates at the UN denouncing Israel. I asked Tom about this.

"Remember, Lance, there are over fifty-seven Islamic states represented in the UN. None of them are willing to recognize a Jewish state. They all want tiny Israel for themselves.

"The Jewish people were promised the land by God, their history took place there, and they redeemed the land. In fact, they bought parcels of land from previous owners, and they cultivated, built it, died for it, and made it come alive. But the Islamic states are greedy. They want to come in and take the fruits all for themselves after others have done the work. They aren't willing to live side-by-side and co-exist with others.

"The Muslim states' territory is over 250 times the size of Israel, from Morocco on the Atlantic all the way across to the doors of India. But, for them, it's not enough. They want everything. Israel is like the size of tiny Rhode Island against, in comparison, an Arab land mass the size of the entire North America. It's just a speck.

"There are one and a half billion Muslims in the world, but only seven million Jews in Israel and, yet, for the Islamic Conference, that is seven million too many! Only the power of God and the determination of the Jewish people to survive in its land have kept the Israelis from being destroyed by Arab countries obsessed in destroying Israel.

"There are other countries that align with the Muslim states against Israel because they're afraid that if they don't, they will be invaded by Muslim terrorists. Some are fearful the Arabs won't sell them oil, while others are bought off or don't seem to have the courage to stand behind one country when fifty-seven others are threatening them. For many, though, it's just become fashionable to condemn Israel."

"Why?" I asked.

"They're envious of Israel's immense success," he answered. "Many Third World countries see how Israel, a relatively young country, has surpassed them in achievement and quality of life. Instead of copying Israel's formula for hard work, advanced education, and deferral of gratification and fun until the job is done, they absolve themselves by wildly condemning Israel and claiming she's not fair. Can there be something 'unfair' about so much creativity and achievement in one tiny place?

"Many Europeans who long ago gave up the rigors of hard work and invention for the comfort of the easy life embodied in the socialist welfare state also condemn Israel for her industry and drive. They find fault with almost everything she does, as do some liberals in America who believe equality means that no person or country should achieve more than anyone else. And, if they do, they must be cheating or guilty of something wrong.

"Indeed, it is conservative Americans who still relish the idea of hard work, sacrifice, innovation, meritocracy, capitalism, and a pick-yourself-up-by-your-bootstraps ethic who admire Israel and cheer her on. Instead of condemning her achievements, they say: 'Let's be like that…and go for it.'

"Success is laudable and something to be proud of if you earned it. It is not something to be demonized. Lance, envy is a sin and corrodes society, and it tries making successful people targets, keeping behind those people mired in it. That's why 'Thou shalt not envy' is written right there in the Ten Commandments."

I thoroughly agreed with him. If everyone in my class wrote reports by simply copying them from the internet, how could any of us learn anything? I know I was learning important things by this conversation with Tom, and I suspect others were too. Our success on our papers would mean something if we worked hard on them.

We had reached Main Street by now and headed over to the square. I was hoping he'd share more with me. This was getting interesting to say the least.

V

We each bought a bottled water at the concession stand and settled ourselves on a bench near the cannon on the north side of the square.

"Sadly," Tom began, "there's another thing at work here. There's a lot of anti-Semitism in the world, and all too many have directed their hatred of Jews onto the State of Israel and to all Jews who support her. For example, many Muslims on American campuses are leading a public campaign to demonize Israel, and they attack Jewish students on campus for wearing a yarmulke, a Jewish star, or even just for looking Jewish. That such anti-Semitism and Islamic bullying is allowed on campus is not only un-American but shows how frightened the college administrators are of Islamic violence and how many of the leftist professors are in favor of hurting Israel and Jews in general. It's called political correctness, which is the right for liberals to hate people and groups who are on a different political side of them.

"It's a cancerous political ideology that allows terrible deeds to be done to those you disagree with by invoking the words, 'social justice.' Because you hold the politically correct position, you are granted license to hurt others.

"This is another reason I support Israel…and so should you. Israel has become the litmus test, the issue dividing those who believe in fair play and objective observation versus those who demonize and feel self-righteous, destroying that which does not mirror their political beliefs.

"Generally, those who dislike Israel also dislike patriotic, historic America and, worse, dislike serious Christianity and fidelity to Scripture, as well as those Evangelicals who live a life of Scripture. Thank God for those called Christian Zionists. They proudly stand behind Israel and stand up to the bullying by the Islamists. Many unfortunately are better supporters of Israel than wayward Jews who have been snared by leftwing political correctness and ideology."

"I haven't paid much attention to politics before, but I think it's time I begin. I'll be voting in the next big election and I just now realized how much I need to learn."

"That's good, Lance. The Christian Zionists have courage and character, qualities I admire, qualities that sustain a civilization. I'm sure you're on board with them. Besides, as many preachers have announced: 'Israel is the only place in the entire Middle East where a Christian can practice his faith and live in peace.' In Muslim lands they are censored, raped, beaten up, plundered, and their Christian symbols are forbidden.

"We know anti-Jewishness is behind much of the hatred for Israel, since the same people who call for boycotting or dismantling Israel because Jews are building apartments in Jerusalem are absolutely silent about the apartheid against Christians in Saudi Arabia, the hangings of Persians and Christians in Iran, the slaughter by Muslims of Christians all over Africa, the terrible human rights violations by communist countries against their citizens, and the dislocation of millions as a consequence of numerous wars around the world.

"When we demand from Jews what we never demand from others, when we demand from Jews impossible requirements, when we criticize any form of self-defense of its people while ignoring the vicious atrocities committed against her by Islamic groups, that's anti-Semitism. It is Jew-hatred dressed up as anti-Israelism or anti-Zionism. Anti-Semitism is the downside of being appointed by God, just as anti-Christianism is the downside of being the target of secularists and Islamists."

Man-oh-man, I was receiving a better education right here on the porch and street corners of Hartford City than I probably will in the quads and classrooms of the campus of Indiana State at Bloomington. Tom didn't seem to be tiring of talking with me, and his blue-grey eyes seemed as fresh now in the early afternoon, as they were back this morning when I first saw him on the bench over at Ebbets Park. He suggested we return back to his Aunt Susan's to see how she was doing. I phoned my mother to let her know where I was, and she mentioned that my sister had just returned from a trip she'd taken to Cincinnati to visit my cousins.

"Just one more thing, Tom. How do these anti-Israel people get away with their naked hate?"

"Ah-ha, now that's the 64 million dollar question. They cover it up by pretending to be concerned by the plight of what they call the 'Palestinians.' As we turned toward Chestnut, he offered me some gum.

"Thanks," I said, taking a stick.

"So here goes," he said. "Ever since the Jews came back en masse to Israel, the surrounding Arab armies have attacked Israel. It's been bad; in fact, during Israel's War of Independence, the Jews had no ammunition, while the departing British had allowed their armaments to be taken and used by the Arabs. The Jewish residents had to improvise, and many starved as the Arabs blockaded cities. But, with the help of God—it was destiny—and great ingenuity and dedication, the Israelis were not defeated. This has happened again and again.

"When realizing that they were not going to defeat the Jewish State, even after a surprise attack against Israel on its holiest day of Yom Kippur, the Arabs came up with a shrewd idea. They said, let's change battlefields. We will beat Israel on the political battlefield. They began insisting that Israel belonged to a people called Palestinians, a group of Arab people who had lived in the area and left during the 1948 Jewish War of Independence. The truth is that the Israelis told their Arab neighbors they should stay and be part of the new State. However, the invading Arab armies told their Arab brethren to leave so that it would be easier for them to bomb and slaughter the Jews inside Israel, and that after the Muslim victory, the Arabs could return and make their own state, a fifty-eighth Arab state.

"But here's the real truth. There is no such thing as an Arab Palestinian nation. This notion of a unique Palestinian people was invented twenty years after Israel had already established a State, fifty years after world diplomats had already researched the whole situation. There was not a Palestinian language, never a mention of it in pre-1948 history books, no particular culture, no flag, no Assembly or formal government—nothing of what normally constitutes a nation. There were simply Arabs from all over the region living in what later was called Israel. Some of them were from Syria, some Lebanon, some from Jordan, some from Egypt. In fact, Yassar Arafat, who claimed to be the Palestinian leader, was born and raised mostly in Egypt; and the family of Mahmud Abbas, the current PLO leader, is actually from Syria, not present day Israel.

"Most of the Arab arrival into what is now Israel came, as I mentioned, from Egypt and Syria which were the principle areas of Islamic culture and life in that region. They are not in-digenous or long-time residents of the Israel territory. The Arabs began coming to the Israel region precisely after the big nineteenth and early twentieth century Jewish immigration to Israel, right after the land began to prosper again after all those vacant centuries.

"The Muslims came to the Israel region for the same reason they're now going to Europe and other modern places around the globe. With the arrival of the Jews, the economy grew sub-stantially and living conditions rose as the Jewish settlers began bringing in electricity, paved roads, sanitation, hospitals, doctors, and all the things of modern life, advances that make life healthier and provide greater economic and educational opportunity and safety. The Jews in Israel, as the Europeans and Americans, provide much safer and secure societies than those found in the wilder, more backward, and unpredictable Muslim countries.

"Most Arabs in the Israel region arrived after the Jews had begun setting up shop. There would have been more Jews than Arabs, but the ruling Turks and later British limited and sometimes forbade Jewish immigration so as not to upset the Arabs. Even today we're experiencing a condition throughout the world where western countries make policies not according to what is right or best for their own citizens, but what they feel is needed not to upset their Muslim population and cause rioting.

"Just as the Arabs are laying claim to Israel, calling themselves the original settlers and brazenly calling the Jews 'occupiers,' one day, when they start gaining big populations in certain European countries, they will similarly I fear, claim the country as theirs and demand that the culture and national symbols be Islamic. They immigrated to the civilized society of Jewish Palestine in the late 1880s and early 1900s and now want to throw out the very people, Jews, who allowed, and even invited, them in the first place. A time-tested Muslim strategy for taking over territory is to accuse those outside Islam of being 'occupiers' in lands that beforehand were not in any way Islamic. Sweden, Holland, Belgium, Spain—watch out!

"Moreover, it was the Jews who were called Palestinians by the ruling British. Most of the Arabs identified with Damascus, not Palestine. Back in 1922, Arab scholars told the League of Nations that there had never been an Arab Palestinian people and they should therefore be granted a different land, the land soon to be called Syria. The Arabs were called Arabs and lived there neither as a nation nor as an identifiable entity, rather as a mixed group of generic Arabs. Most Arabs never saw themselves as part of a particular nation but rather as Muslims; for in

Muslim outlook, nationhood is a modern invention against their more important belief in Muslimhood, what they call the *ummah*.

"Names such as Iraq, Jordan, Saudi Arabia, and Syria did not exist as national names until so assigned by the British. Neither did the name 'Palestine' connect to anything Muslim. There was no people called Palestinians, except perhaps the Jews whose passports read Palestine. Palestine is, as I mentioned before, a Roman name, a name given to the Davidic Commonwealth by Rome in the year 135 A.D. when the land was entirely Jewish.

"And here's the kicker: throughout the short time that Jordan ruled the area of Israel west of the Jordan River, known by some as the West Bank, the Muslim Arabs who lived there never called themselves Palestinians, nor did they clamor for a state of their own or demand that Jordan make a Palestinian state in that area. Only when Israel won back that land from Jordan did the Arabs claim the land as belonging to a Palestinian nation.

"That is why during all the years they resided there, the Arabs hardly developed the land or built thriving cities, institutions, or bountiful farms in contrast to the Israelis. They didn't build a nation there because there had never been a Palestinian nation to rebuild. A genuine nation would have given devotion and tenderness to the land it claimed was their ancestral home. They didn't because it isn't."

My head was now spinning. What misconceptions most of us can have when we don't know the real facts!

"One of the reasons Israelis find land within Judea and Samaria to build cities, what some call settlements, is that the Arabs never cultivated these lands and, like no-man's lands, left these huge tracts of land uninhabited and un-farmed. These areas belonged to nobody. The Jews, however, love the land and want to bring out its potential, fulfill the promise of the land, so that this sacred earth can be the best it can be. Just because an Arab had a cottage on a specific lot does not entitle him to all the square miles around it. No one can claim the land that is miles around their home if indeed they have not bought it or shown a deed of ownership or improvements on that parcel. Since post-biblical times, these areas have been owned by no specific country or nation. Arabs have no presumed right to it.

"Muslims and Arabs buy land and houses in Israel. I've seen it with my own eyes. The world would not accept the outlawing of buying land or homes by an Arab in Israel. Likewise, the Arabs have no right to deny Jews property in Judea and Samaria, especially since Judea and Samaria were historically and definitely Jewish and have only recently been disputed. If Arabs are free to settle, so are Jews.

"There are some neighborhoods around Jerusalem that were previously Arab and are now Jewish. But the Arabs sold those houses and received payment. No one forced them to sell. Vice versa, in many parts of the Galilee, Arabs have bought Jewish homes. No one seems to think that by buying Jewish houses, Arabs are usurping Jewish property and neighborhoods and acting as 'occupiers or settlers.' It's commerce. It happens every day, everywhere in the world. It's the reality of real estate. Many neighborhoods in Brooklyn and Manhattan, for example, that were owned by blacks for the last 70 years are now owned by whites; they are trendy places where blacks have sold out and received trendy prices. There are also neighborhoods that were once white and are now black. People buy and sell, homes fluctuate, neighborhoods change.

"Unfortunately, the world seems to be acceding to the Islamic belief that once Islamic, a country, city, neighborhood, or house must always remain Islamic, while non-Islamic places must be 100% open to Islam. By so doing, we are allowing ourselves to be shorted of our own civil rights and dignity. It's what Muslims call *dhimmitude*, treating non-Muslims as second class.

Well, Israelis cannot allow themselves to be dhimmis in their own country. Israelis are not 'occupiers.' You can't be an occupier in your own land. The Jews are owners.

"Lance, about 40 years ago a very wise and far-sighted person stressed how honest and truth-seeking people must counter the lies the Arab/Muslim community is spreading regarding their purported ownership of the land west of the Jordan River; if not, Arabs will begin manufacturing even bigger lies to advance their goals. And just like he said, it has happened and is continuing to happen."

"Can you give me some examples?" I asked. I didn't know this was happening and was eager to hear the details.

"Yes. They began saying that God gave them the land and that Jerusalem belongs to them. They went even further and said there never was a Jewish Temple built on the Temple Mount. They even denied the existence of Solomon and David. They have gone so far as to say they are the real Jewish people. These are, of course, some of the biggest, grossest lies of all time; but, as the Nazi Goebbels said: 'If you repeat a lie often enough, people start to believe it, especially if it's a big and preposterous lie.' People figure that no one would actually be brazen enough to claim a BIG lie and look like a fool, so there must be truth to it."

I guess Tom is right. I remembered some of the lies told among my classmates along the way. They were always found out in the end, but many of the kids fell for them.

"Now, we who believe the Bible know there was a King David and King Solomon and that David founded Jerusalem as the capital of ancient Israel and had drawn plans to build a Temple to God, what in biblical Hebrew is called *Beit Ha'Mikdash*. We know how Solomon, his son, actually did build it in on the mount originally called Moriah.

"Unfortunately even as we speak, Muslims are purposely digging under the Temple Mount and destroying all evidence—

coins, pots, pans, and other items—depicting Jewish Temple life of long ago. That is why supporting Israel and her right to the land are absolutely important to you as a Bible believing Christian. Islam is asserting that its Koran version of history is correct and the Bible's version—Old and New Testament—is wrong."

Wow, I thought to myself. I had never thought of this point before. Yes, this whole issue of who has the right to the land is Islam's push and demand that their Koran is the truth and thus Islam is the religion of truth. It's more than just a political question but goes to the heart of whose Holy Book is correct—theirs or ours.

And if the Muslim version of history is correct, then our whole understanding and belief in Jesus is put at risk. After all, Jesus and the New Testament rest on the preceding truth of the Jewish Bible, Isaiah, and the Gospels themselves. Islam's ambition for Israel is part of its religious war of supremacy over Judaism and Christianity. Yes, this matters to me! Very much.

If Islam's Koran is correct, then all Christians and Jews are supposed to be dhimmi, second class and subservient to Islam and Muslims. Yes, this is very personal. Supporting Israel is no longer just a political question or one of justice or accurate history, but one involving my personal survival, the survival of my church, and the survival of the family I hope one day to have.

"Lance," he continued, "look how ludicrous their claims are. They call themselves the real Jews, yet they follow the Koran and not the Torah. It is the Jews that have followed the Torah and until this day celebrate Passover, Pentecost, Tabernacles, and the biblical holidays. The Muslims celebrate Ramadan, something not mentioned in the Bible.

"It is the Jews who 'bind their arm and wear frontlets between their eyes as signs between God and Israel.' It is the Jews who have prayed three times a day for 2500 years, and still do, for everlasting attachment to Israel and Jerusalem. The Muslims pray to Mecca. Jews pray to the biblical Jehovah, Adonai. Muslims worship Allah.

"Ask the Babylonians who destroyed the first Temple and the Romans who destroyed the second Temple. They didn't fight Mohammed but Judah. They didn't destroy the Muslim mosque but the Jewish Temple in Jerusalem. Only Muslims, atheists, or downright haters of Jews could fall for this bizarre propaganda saying there was no David, Solomon, Covenant, and Jewish Temple, or that the Jewish people are not the real Jewish people. Anyone prizing intellectual honesty must stand against these lies. Supporting Israel is important to me because it means I am a person of truth who will not be caught up in a mass movement, a frenzy, to accept blatant, historic falsehoods. I have too much integrity for that."

Integrity. Yes, he was a man of integrity. I could see that. I wanted to be like that too. We started heading back to Mrs. McCray's house, both of us lost in our own thoughts.

VI

"Tom," I asked after we had gone a few blocks, "do you have time to quote me some Scripture, some passages from the Bible about God's promise to the Jewish people about the land? After all, Ishmael was also a son of Abraham."

"Sure," he answered. "There are dozens of references, but let me just give you a few. Yes, Abraham had a son with Hagar named Ishmael. But Hagar was a concubine, not a wife. The promised son was Isaac, who was born of Abraham and his wife, Sarah, the marriage from which the promises and covenant were made. Abraham's covenanted family was established with Sarah and their offspring. Isaac's birth was the special, ordained birth. The three messengers from God, the angels, who came many years after Ishmael had already been born, came to deliver the specific Good News regarding the upcoming birth and destiny residing in Isaac. 'In Isaac shall your seed be called,' God says to Abraham (Genesis 21:13). This repeats what was stated in Genesis 17:19, 'Thou shall call your son Isaac and I will establish my Covenant with him everlasting, and with his seed after him.' God knew to repeat that which he feared would be challenged in the future, centuries later."

And Sarah witnessed how the son of Hagar, the concubine from Egypt, was mocking, acting with impurity (Genesis 21:9).

And so Abraham gave his inheritance to Isaac. To his children from his concubines he gave gifts and sent them away from Isaac, while he, Abraham, was still alive. He sent them to lands eastward, to lands east of Canaan (Genesis 25:5-6).

And Ishmael dwelt in the desert of Havilah, which is Arabia that is before Egypt (Genesis 25:18).

And God appeared to Isaac and said dwell in this Land and I will be with you and bless you. For to you and your children after you will I give this Land as I swore to Abraham your father (Genesis 26:2-4).

"Isaac, not Ishmael, is the custodian of the land. We need to believe that, for as the verse continues:

And in thy seed, Isaac, shall all the nations of the earth be blessed (Genesis 26:4).

"The promise and blessing continues with Isaac's son, Jacob."

And the Lord stood above and to Jacob He declared: I am the God of your father Abraham and God of Isaac. The Land upon which you rest shall I give to you and your children thereafter (Genesis 28:13).

"By then, Ishmael is completely out of the picture. The covenant continued and was reiterated with Moses. At the Burning Bush, God tells Moses:

I am the God of your fathers, Abraham, Isaac and Jacob. I have seen the affliction of my People. I will go down and deliver them from Egypt and bring them up to the Land flowing with milk and honey, the Land where now reside the Canaanites (Exodus 3:6, 8).

"Later, God warns Moses and the Israelites not to make treaties with the inhabitants within the land."

Take heed to thyself and do not make treaties with the inhabitants of this land where you will settle, for they will be a continuous thorn and snare in your midst (Exodus 34:12).

Rely on God and your strength, not the feigned peace-making treaties of your enemies. "Do not make a treaty with them [Philistines] or their gods" (Exodus 24:32).

"Before his death, Moses again declares:

Love your God and listen to His voice. For He is the life and length of your days in the Land that the Lord promised to your fathers Abraham, Isaac and Jacob, to give them (Deut. 30:20).

"God keeps giving the land to the Jewish people and fulfilling his Promise. God renews the Covenant with Moses' successor, Joshua."

After the death of Moses, God spoke unto Joshua, saying: Moses my servant is dead. Arise; go over the Jordan, thou and thy people unto the Land which I give to them the Children of Israel (Joshua 1:1-2).

"The land west of the Jordan is Jewish land. Let's fast forward to years later."

And it came to pass that David inquired of the Lord. And the Lord said unto him, Go up. And David asked: Whither? And He said: Hebron. And they made David king in Hebron (II Samuel 2:1, 4).

"Hebron is in the Judean part of Judea and Samaria, referred to by diplomats as the West Bank. Hebron is the city of the Cave of the Machpelah, where Abraham and Sarah, Isaac and Rebecca, and Jacob and Leah are buried. Not Ishmael."

So all the elders came before the Lord and they anointed David King of Hebron. And he reigned in Hebron for 7 years and thereafter in Jerusalem for 33 years, over Israel and Judah (II Samuel 5:4-5).

"For thou has established thy people Israel," says David, *"to be thy nation forever and be their God. The Lord of hosts is the God of Israel and the House of David is established before thee. And I will build thee a House, a Temple; and with thy blessing let the House of thy servant be blessed forever"* (II Samuel 7:24-27, 29).

"Yes, it is a fact that David lived, he was King of Israel, and had plans to build God's Temple in Jerusalem."

And David reigned over all Israel and executed judgment and justice unto its entire people (II Samuel 8:15).

And behold, I [Solomon] will build a House, a Temple, unto the Lord, as was said unto my father David (I Kings 5:19).

And it came to pass in the 480th year after the children of Israel came out of the land of Egypt, in the fourth year of Solomon's reign, that he began building the House of the Lord (I Kings 6:1).

Then Solomon assembled the elders of Israel, the heads of the tribes, and the children of Israel unto King Solomon in Jerusalem that they bring up the Ark of the Covenant to the City of David, which is Zion (I Kings 8:1).

There was something that was still bothering me. "What about the fact that the Jews were exiled out of Israel twice? Does that nullify their right to the land?" I asked Tom.

"Absolutely not; these exiles were already foretold as well as the Jewish people's eventual return. Moses, while still in the desert, alerted the Children of Israel that, because of certain sins, they would be temporarily exiled (Deut. 30:18). Every Jew who lived after Sinai knew of what is written in Leviticus 26— there would be an exile; and later, in Deuteronomy 26, there's a warning of a second exile. Sin. Too many began disregarding the Commandments and some followed blindlessly without passion.

"Quite often a casual commitment to God's commandments leads to hedonism. Preoccupation with pleasures too often leads to military weakness and invites conquest from the outside. With the loss of religious identity, a nation stops taking itself seriously and begins diminishing the importance of protecting itself, placing national self-defense as a secondary issue. Without religion, a nation loses its distinctiveness, and in its new-found transnationalism believes its security lies in being like everyone else and disregards a strong national defense. These same sins are what we are seeing today in America, conditions that lead to weakness and, like Rome, invite conquest.

"The first exile lasted 70 years, the second 1,700 years. But God equally promised: 'I will return you from the four corners of the earth back to your Land.' Even so, there never was a period throughout any of the exiles when the land was absent a Jewish presence. It may have been a small one, yes, but there was a remaining remnant nonetheless, maintaining a national and spiritual foothold. More importantly, during the periods of exile, Jews imparted the themes and message of the Torah to their surroundings and received from these new lands and people wisdom, important teachings, and attitudes.

"It is precisely these two exiles that make the Jewish return more dramatic and, unquestionably, divine. Who would have believed such a thing possible? Who would have believed the prophecies of Israel's return, so beautifully announced in Jeremiah, Ezekiel, Isaiah, Zachariah, and Daniel? Who could have believed that a people as weak and impoverished as the Jewish people during their centuries of torment in Europe and Arabia would have been able to return, rebuild, and spawn rebirth to an ancient land? Only God could have pulled off such a feat, verifying that what some had thought was merely fanciful dreams became actual fact. Israel's return proves and affirms the Bible's veracity. Non-believers, of course, will scoff at or try to overturn anything that manifests God's Word or his will."

Now that answered my question. I was getting a better understanding of the truth about the exiles.

"The Jews who returned reinstituted the biblical language of Hebrew, a language in which they prayed and studied throughout their exile. The Muslims speak Arabic. Arabic is not the biblical language, nor was it ever the language of the biblical people.

Remember Jacob and Israel, for thou are my servant. Israel thou shall not be forgotten by me. I have blotted out thine transgressions. I have redeemed thee. The Lord hath redeemed Jacob and glorified himself in Israel. It is said to Jerusalem. Thou shall be inhabited; and to the cities of Judah, Ye shall be rebuilt, and I will raise up the decayed places thereof (Isaiah 44:21-26).

And he said: Thou shall be my servant to raise up the tribes of Jacob and to restore the preserved of Israel (Isaiah 49:6).

Sing and rejoice, O daughter of Zion: for lo, I come, and I will dwell in the midst of thee, says the Lord (Zachariah 3:14, 16).

"Isaiah and God extol and rejoice in Zion along with those who long for Zion, who are known as the Zionists. In contrast, the Arab and Muslim world, along with the politically left/liberal world, curse the Zionists and the Zionists' dream. Lance, join with the Zionists, for your reward will be great. 'And many nations shall be joined to the Lord that day and shall be my people' (Isaiah 3:15). Be from those people, from those who subscribe to this Book and these prophecies, not those books that come to defy it."

Thus sayeth the Lord: I am returned unto Zion and will dwell in the midst of Jerusalem. And Jerusalem shall be called the City of Truth, and the mount the Holy Mount. There shall the old men and women dwell in the streets of Jerusalem and her streets shall be full of boys and girls playing. Behold, I shall save my people from the land of the east country and the land of the west Country. And I shall bring them and they shall dwell in the midst of Jerusalem; and they shall be my people and I will be their God (Isaiah 8:3-8).

"With the rebirth of the State of Israel by those pioneering Jews from western and eastern Europe and eastern Babylon and Persia who called themselves Zionists, the land is once again thriving and full of joy. In Jerusalem's Jewish Quarter in the Old

City, you'll see children for the first time in almost 2,000 years playing and laughing. Nowhere in the Koran is there talk of rebuilding Jerusalem or associating God with Zion. A Jerusalem resurrected by God is the City of Truth.

"Lance, do the right thing and make sure America does the right thing."

> *And it shall come to pass in that day that I will seek to destroy all the nations that come against Jerusalem. But on the house of David and upon the inhabitants of Jerusalem I shall pour my spirit of grace* (Zachariah 12:9-10).

"Speak to your congressman and your friends about supporting Zion, Israel. Make sure that America remains on the side of Israel. Until now it has, but there are some dangerous signs, some people in high-up positions here who no longer identify with Israel. They are on the side of the Arabs and Muslims.

"We need your generation of young people to counter and stand against the never-ending hostile push by newly arrived Muslims. They bully and intimidate students and staff in local high schools and college by demonizing Israel and whitewashing the cruel and barbaric acts going on in too many Islamic countries and societies. I know it's hard to stand against the trendy, hip-hop tide, but I know you can do it. Many of your valiant friends will follow your example."

VII

At this point I was getting some good ideas for my report and how I could tie it all up with challenging the students to learn all they could about what was going on in the world today.

For the sake of Zion I will not be silent; and for the sake of Jerusalem, I will not rest. No longer shall forsaken be said of you, and desolate shall no longer be said of your Land. You shall be called 'My desire in her' and your Land inhabited, for the Lord desires you and that your land be inhabited (Isaiah 62:1, 4).

Tom began again: "When these prophecies were announced over 2500 years ago, who would have believed that the desolate land would flourish, be made robust and fruitful as it has since 1948? Zechariah: 2:16 says: 'And the Lord will take Judah into his possessions as his portion on the holy soil and will choose Jerusalem forever.' In other words: one, undivided, original Jerusalem.

"Some people errantly think the Arabs had a nation there from way back because they look the part. After all, the men dress how it was done years ago, with flowing gowns and kufiyahs, and use donkeys, the way we envision ancient shepherds dressing and riding. The Jews, on the other hand, dress in pants, suits, ties, and drive cars. But that's all superficial movie stuff. It's the history and dedication that counts, and that's Jewish, from way back. In fact, ancient and historical Israel was never part of the nomadic Arabian Desert landscape; it was a Mediterranean enclave, more akin to the atmosphere of Greece, Rome, and ancient Alexandria than Arabia and the Sahara.

"If the Muslims in the region want a state, they have one in the country of Jordan. That was the state the British carved out specifically to answer the demands for an Arabic state near Palestine. You see, originally, with the Balfour Declaration of 1917, the ruling British decided that the land between the Mediterranean to Mesopotamia (near present day Iraq), should be called Palestine and be given to the Jews for their new state. The remaining millions of square miles in the Mideast would be given to Arab/Muslim entities and divided into new kingdoms. Up to that point, these lands were mere non-demarcated spaces run by tribes. Thus, the Jews were supposed to live in an area five times larger than what they actually have today.

"The Arabs were unhappy, so they began rioting, what they call an *intifada*, and bullied the British into dividing Palestine in half by creating a new country called Trans-Jordan, its territory being from across the Jordan River eastward to Mesopotamia, settling all the Arabs of the region within that boundary. There would now be a West Palestine for the Jews, from the Mediterranean until the Jordan River, and an East Palestine called Trans-Jordan for the Arabs. Though it meant a huge cut of 77% from the original mandate promised the Jews, they reluctantly agreed.

"Yes, the Jews, ever seeking peaceful co-existence, agreed. They were not greedy. Besides, as the world convinced them, a country between the Mediterranean on one side and the Jordan River on the other was logical and seemed to be a natural geographic unity of land.

"But when Israel declared its independence, not only did the Arabs remain unsatisfied with the Trans-Jordan they were given, but they wanted all of Israel. They waged war and captured much of the West Bank, the land west of the Jordan River originally called Judea and Samaria, its Jewish biblical names. The British and world maps, in fact, called these districts Judea and Samaria. The Arabs conquered portions of Judea and Samaria and ended up with a staggering, disproportionate 82% of the land originally mandated to the Jewish people in the

Balfour Declaration. The original intent of the League of Nations plan had been turned upside down, due to unyielding Muslim belligerence.

"Something similar happened after the British left India. India is a majority Hindu country. There are Muslims there as well—a minority—but they want India. So they intifada'd there. In order to stop the rioting, the world leaned on India and cut 1/3 from it and made Pakistan. The Arabs saw that rioting worked—violence always seems to do so for them—and the world asked India to now give up land on its other side, which became Muslim Bangladesh. Still unsatisfied, the Muslims wish to now take Kashmir from India.

"A fearful and short-sighted western world seems to always pressure countries to give in to Islamic territorial power grabs. They know they can pressure western states but never Islamic states. Islamic states and groups don't compromise on territory or religious control. It is a grim reality we must face as Islam keeps marching forward and taking lands all over the world from indigenous populations. Thankfully many in Israel and America are no longer naïve to the long-term imperialistic goals of Islam.

"The Arabs want to shrink Israel piecemeal until it no longer exists. No doubt about it. They already have 80% of the original land that had been set aside for Israel. Now they want the entire Israeli West Bank of Judea and Samaria. But everyone knows that Hamas and Fatah will make a terrorist state out of it, a launching pad against Israel, where they'll reign down rockets on her just as they did from Gaza after the Israelis gave it to them for their Muslim Palestinian state.

"In fact, the Muslims within the West Bank will never know freedom if the Israelis leave. They will be wards of a Hamas, or an Iranian terror state. The Arabs most safe and protected from the Islamic tyranny and terrorism rampaging throughout the Mideast are the ones within Israeli jurisdiction.

"More than anything, the Muslims want Jerusalem, Israel's eternal capital, founded by David and built to the glory of God by Solomon. The Arabs know that whoever owns Jerusalem can lay claim to all of Israel. For Zion is Jerusalem. Some Europeans want to give the Arabs control of Jerusalem so as to protect themselves from terror in their European cities. By pleasing the Muslims at the expense of the Jews, the Europeans think they are buying safety from Islamic terrorism. Others want Israel to cede her capital because they wish to strip Israel of her identity and glory, hoping that such will precipitate Israel's eventual slide into oblivion, or as a state the size of a Tel Aviv beach.

"Beyond doubt, the goal of a Palestinian state is not democracy but to become a base to destroy Israel, the Jewish state. Many of the PLO and Hamas leaders jubilantly talk of imposing another Holocaust on the Jews of Israel and Jews worldwide. For many Arabs, the Hitler Holocaust against the Jews was simply Phase One, while finishing the job against Israel is Phase Two, the Final Destruction.

"We can't let that happen," Tom continued in a louder voice. "We must stand and defend historical truth. If we won't stick behind Israel, what will happen one day when Islam claims they, not Columbus, discovered America? After all, they've already changed the name of Constantinople, the seat of Byzantine Christianity, to Istanbul and are now trying to brainwash us into believing Jesus was not Jewish but an Arab Palestinian. But all intellectually honest people know that Jesus was Jewish, not an Arab. He was not a Palestinian either. The word had not yet been coined during Jesus' lifetime. His genealogy was Jewish as were his religious and spiritual roots. He was a real rabbi, not some Imam. This inaccuracy is being peddled not only by Muslims but also by some wayward Christian leaders wanting to form a new alliance between Christianity and Islam that they call 'Chrislam.' This Islamic propaganda is a fight not only against Israel but conventional Christianity as well."

VIII

It was already early evening and time to get home for dinner, but I had one very important question I needed answered before I left. "So how do the Arab Muslims create sympathy for their cause, how are they able to make themselves the poor victims?" I really wanted to know.

"They do so," Tom answered quietly, "by keeping thousands of their Arab brothers and sisters, entire families, inside makeshift refugee camps. They have been doing this for three generations. They don't let their people out. They cram them inside these camps and bring people from around the world, the U.N., from the E.U., and leftwing activists, and parade their brothers and sisters around as pitiful victims of Israeli 'occupation.'

"But none of them have to live in such conditions. Look at the beautiful houses and villas throughout the West Bank built by Arabs who call themselves Palestinian leaders or are relatives of the leaders or workers and business operatives in the 'cause.' I've seen them. Most of them live better than the Israelis.

"Nothing is stopping these refugees from moving out, except one thing: their Arab/Muslim overlords who force them inside the camps so that first, the worldwide money to help the Arabs keeps flowing into the wallets and secret bank accounts of the Muslim leaders. And second, they want to keep world pressure on Israel to relinquish Judea and Samaria and their cities within the West Bank, along with Jerusalem. Theirs is a never-ending campaign to delegitimize the entire state and existence of Israel. Their goal is no Israel.

"Unfortunately, those in leftwing circles who want to think the worst of Israel now have the narrative and photos they've been hoping for in order to paint the false picture they want. What's even more cynical than this is the fact that the wealthy Arab oil-producing countries, always crying about their Palestinian brothers, have enough spare money to feed, clothe, house, and educate every single one of them. They don't, of course. They don't want the problem solved. They don't want their Arab brothers. They don't care about their Arab brothers. Yet no one points to them as hard-hearted or exploiters of fellow Arabs. And that is because deep down it's not about the welfare of the Palestinians but the delegitimizing of Israel by Muslims, anti-Semites, leftists, and the envious.

"Israel can't be accused of 'occupation.' You can't be an 'occupier' in your own land. Truth be told, the Muslim Arabs are the occupiers. That's the biblical and historic truth, that's the truth based on who revived the land and who rebuilt it.

"What about Israel's achievements? Much of the leftwing western world would rather deprive themselves of Israeli inventions for a better life than see the Jews succeed. Well, not all. Every time an Arab has a medical problem, he rushes to an Israeli hospital to be cured and saved. Some have come back and repaid the good deed by attempting a suicide bombing against the hospital staff. That's the evil mindset of jihadism."

How sickening, I thought. "What do you think the media's role in all this has been, Tom?"

"For most of the media, taking the side of Islam has become the 'romantic' thing to do. They foolishly think they are defending the weak and downtrodden. It makes them feel morally superior. It's mind boggling. But never underestimate the sway of vanity over people. So, now you know the rest of the story. I bet you never expected to hear all this when you asked your first question."

"Hey, no I didn't. But this has been good. I have lots of material not just for my report but for my life."

"Just one more thing," Tom suddenly remarked. "Lance,

something is happening in the world today that is making it exceedingly difficult for Israel to even defend herself. They are being indicted even when making a protection wall as a buffer against incoming Islamic suicide bombers."

"Go on," I encouraged him.

"All over the world today, Muslims are attacking, beating, hacking, and axing citizens in Europe, America, Australia—you name it. But most western leaders don't have the stomach or belief in their own culture or nationhood to clamp down on these aggressive and hostile communities within their own country. They fear being called 'Islamophobic,' the new term used to silence us. Worse, many of the liberal politicians rely on the votes of the Islamic community in their midst to get elected. So they deliberately ignore their Islamic problem and pretend it doesn't exist.

"Every time a Muslim man kills an American citizen, President Obama, for example, rushes out to tell us 'Islam is a religion of peace.' Others blame us westerners for not understanding and not listening enough to Islamic never-ending grievances. We are accused of being 'provocative' simply when exercising the Bill of Rights' First Amendment of Freedom of Speech, applying local customs and zoning laws when trying to stop demographic neighborhood aggression, or simply protecting ourselves. All this, of course, is an undignified appeasement from our politicians.

"When Israel defends herself against Islamic terrorism—as it must—instead of the Europeans congratulating Israel for protecting its people and enjoying survival, the Europeans denounce Israel. They don't want to commend Israel for doing the very thing they are afraid to do in their own countries. They don't want their own appeasement and weakness spotlighted, so instead, they'll assert there's no Islamic problem, just an Israeli problem. They'll shift the blame onto Israel."

"But how can the Europeans and leftists in America deny the terrorism from Islam against Israel?" I wondered.

"They do so by saying it's not Islamic terrorists but 'Palestinian freedom fighters.' They justify this terrorism. For others, such as President Obama, the French, The Hague, Belgium, and even some in Britain and Sweden, the dislike of Jewish Israel is so intense they purposely deny any Islamic problem in their own country so that Israel is unable to speak of its corresponding Islamic problem, a problem requiring a serious and strong self-defense. They never admit that Israel is on the frontlines against Islam's march against the west.

"The upshot is that in order that Israel not be exonerated for her war against Palestinian terrorism, Europeans will say Islam is no real problem. By so doing, they leave their own societies vulnerable to an Islamic takeover of their countries. They are committing suicide. Their own Jew hatred will result in their self-inflicted demise."

We reached Mrs. McCray's house and I could smell fish broiling. "Would you like to stay for dinner?" she asked me. "We have red snapper, red potatoes, broccoli, and Boston Cream Pie for desert. Fisher's Supermarket had a sale today on snapper."

"No, thanks, I'd better be going home. My mother has dinner for us. My sister just came back from Cincinnati. Tom, what time is your train tomorrow?"

"I'm scheduled to leave on the afternoon 1:25."

"Well, Tom, I don't know if I'll see you again. It was sure great talking to you. I learned a lot. Tons."

We shook hands as we warmly bid each other goodbye. What a great guy, I thought. Tom led me out to the screen door, gave me a pat on the back and off I went up Chestnut toward my home on Reynolds Ave., about a fifteen minute walk.

After dinner, I went upstairs and decided no matter what, I'd get to the station tomorrow to see Tom off. I owed him so much. He gave up most of his day and vacation time here for me.

I enjoyed his company, and while learning about Israel from

him, I also learned a lot about the great battles facing the world and how difficult it can be to buck the fashionable trends to support the right side.

Many people think that if you are successful, you must have been lucky or cheated to get there; and if you aren't successful, you must be a victim or someone too noble for us to expect hard work on a consistent basis. The truth is often people are successful precisely because they follow the golden rule and work hard, while people often fail because they'd rather be a victim or live by a set of principles that lead to nowhere. I'm glad we in America and Israel live by biblical Judeo-Christian principles. They are worth living by and fighting for.

IX

The next afternoon, I made it to the train station in time. Tom was there with a small suitcase, wearing his linen jacket, striped tie, and a fresh light blue cotton shirt. He looked pleased to see me.

"I had to see you off," I said.

"I appreciate your coming," Tom responded, and it truly seemed he meant it. "You know," he continued, "there's something I thought of after you left yesterday that I hadn't mentioned and hoped to do so today if I saw you again."

We sat down on one of the benches and Tom began: "People sometimes think that the Israelis are a Goliath and the Arabs like David the underdog. That's not so. The Israelis have a productive society because they try harder and gear their lives towards positive things and not destruction or suicide killings. The Israelis are the underdog. Much of the world is against them. Their country is small, and they are but a few millions in number compared to the billions among their enemy.

"Nobody funds the Israelis; the entire left wing, most of academia, the media, and the powerful NGO groups are against them. The World Bank, the European Union, the Obama administration, Arab monarchs, and others unendingly bankroll and fund the Muslims in the West Bank with mega billions and really, no strings attached. The only difference between the situation now in 2015 and before in 1939-1946 when Germany was arrayed against the Jewish people, is that now the Jews have an army in Israel. And to survive now, they always have to remain one step ahead militarily. That is why the entire Muslim and leftwing world wants to stop Israel's military from defending Israel by concocting so-called war crimes. Israel remains like

David, small and alone; but instead of only having a slingshot, Israel has a real army. It is the Muslim world with its billions of people, its billions of dollars, and its backing by both the U.N. and leftists in Europe and America that is Goliath. The Muslim world is also Goliath in its ideology and its war against Jehovah, the God of the Bible.

"Sticking up for Israel is standing by the principles we believe in. In today's political climate, it takes unusual courage to support her. It shows character and a deep commitment to what's right vs. what's wrong and dangerously trendy. Israel is at the center of the war for our civilization.

"If God forbid, they lose, then we lose. If we lose, we are in for a terrible era of darkness. This battle is the age-old battle of God vs. paganism, decency vs. jihadism, classic values vs. a clever barbarism concealed in the face of victimhood. Lance, those of us who choose Israel thereby choose life."

He smiled at me and rose as he heard the whistle of the approaching train. "I guess my train is almost here. I have really enjoyed our conversation. Thanks for listening."

"Tom, how do you say 'friend' in Hebrew?"

"Chaver," he answered.

"How do you say goodbye and good wishes?"

"Shalom," he answered, this time with a smile.

I looked at Tom and said, "Shalom Chaver."

"Shalom Chaver to you too, Lance."

Shalom. The train was now in the station, ready to be boarded. Tom went up the few stairs to the coach, entered the train, looked back, and waved.

"All aboard!" the conductor shouted out. Soon the doors closed, and the train slowly pulled out of the Hartford City station, heading towards its next destination. As it picked up speed, I watched it disappear around the bend. Surprising myself, I felt emotional. I thought, Shalom Chaver. God bless you. Shalom, my friend for life.

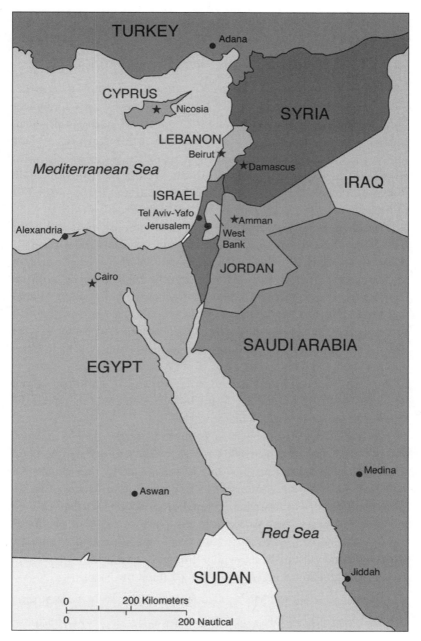

It's Not About Land
Israel occupies less than .2% of the area of the Middle East!

Our Commitment to the Jewish People and Israel
A Message from Mike and Mickey Gottfried

We hope that you have enjoyed reading *Why Israel Matters to You* by our good friend, Aryeh Spero. We met Aryeh by divine appointment while working together, along with our friend Aaron Früh, on an initiative to support Israel <http://youtu.be/mPtZqkqiA9E>. Many ministries and leaders came together at that time for a national press conference to declare, in an open letter to Prime Minister Benjamin Netanyahu, "Israel, You're Not Alone." This declaration appeared in full-page ads in *The Wall Street Journal* and *The Jerusalem Post.*

Israel is being pressured by the Obama administration and the U.S. State Department to give up land and make other concessions. Almost every day we read in the news, stories of the persecution of Jews around the world. Events foretold in the Bible are playing out in front of us. Iran is close to a nuclear weapon and they fund Hamas and Hezbollah, the sworn enemies of Israel. We must be watchman on the wall. Christians can support Israel by praying for its leaders, Prime Minister Benjamin Netanyahu, and the Jewish people. We bless Israel and ask the Lord daily to put a hedge of protection around the borders of Israel. As God said to Abraham in Genesis 12:3, "I will bless those who bless you, and I will curse him who curses you; and in you all the families of the earth shall be blessed." (NKJV)

As a ministry, Team Focus is committed to the people of Israel and her land. It is our heartfelt hope that God's mercy will be upon the nation of Israel during this time of worldwide threats against her very existence. We are committed to the mandate of Psalm 122:6 to, "Pray for the peace of Jerusalem: 'May they prosper who love you.'"

It is our desire that we enlarge the place of our tent (Is. 54:2) through this book. Our purpose is to encourage Christians to support the people and land of Israel, which God gave to Abraham, Isaac and Jacob, through earnest prayer and taking a stand for Israel.

—Shalom, Mike and Mickey Gottfried, co-founders of Team Focus

For Zion's sake I will not keep silent, for Jerusalem's sake I will not remain quiet, till her vindication shines out like the dawn, her salvation like a blazing torch (Isaiah 62:1 NIV).

Also see: http://youtu.be/v-Zm10BCyxc

About the Author

Aryeh Spero's articles have appeared in *The Wall Street Journal, The Washington Times, National Review, Human Events, Townhall, American Thinker, Jerusalem Post* and numerous publications across the country. He has been interviewed on *Fox News* by Bill O'Reilly, Steve Doocy on *Fox and Friends*, and by Neil Cavuto, Megyn Kelly, Bill Hemmer, and Stuart Varney, and is a member of the Faith Panel seen on Gretchen Carlson's *The Real Story*. His interviews on radio include Laura Ingraham, Michael Savage, Dennis Miller, Jim Bohannon, Dick Morris, Tom Marr, Barry Farber, and he is regularly featured on talk radio regarding morality and culture. He has appeared on the Glenn Beck TV program, writes on faith issues for *The Blaze*, and is a contributor to *CNS News*. Spero has testified before Congress and spoken at a meeting of the National Press Club. He has served congregations in Ohio, Manhattan, and Long Island. He's a devoted husband and father.

Spero has been invited to speak to policy makers, candidates, and elected officials regarding the moral and religious dimensions of proposed legislation and by colleges regarding the morality of capitalism. In the mid-1990s he co-founded a conservative think tank of Black and Jewish political conservatives and is a highly regarded and inspiring speaker. He was the first rabbi to endorse Ronald Reagan for President in public newspaper ads around the country.

Contact information:

To contact Aryeh Spero, go to his website at:

caucusforamerica.com or phone 212-252-6861

Also visit: pushbackamerica.com

Other Resources
Several excellent books for further reading:

Push Back—Reclaiming the American Judeo-Christian Spirit
by Rabbi Aryeh Spero ISBN 978-1-58169-455-0

Two Minute Warning by Coach Bill McCartney and Aaron Früh
ISBN 978-1-93526-500-9

Biblical Zionism Series by Rev. Malcolm Hedding:
    The Basis of Christian Support for Israel ISBN 978-0-9765297-0-5
    The Heart of Biblical Zionism ISBN 978-0-9765297-1-2
    The Great Covenants of the Bible ISBN 978-0-9765297-2-9
    The New Testament & Israel ISBN 978-0-9765297-3-6
    Available from ICEJ Publications: www.icejusa.org

Hatred of the Jew by Victor Schlatter ISBN 978-1-58169-576-2
(Spring 2015 release)

About Team Focus

Team Focus was founded in 2000 by Coach Mike Gottfried and his wife, Mickey, to strengthen the family by filling the "father gap." Mike's vision is based on his own life experience of having to grow up without a father, when at the age of 11 his father died. "Growing up without a father around and knowing what it feels like, I have a desire to provide a place for young men to come and be encouraged, motivated, and challenged."

The primary goal of Team Focus is to provide young men, ages 10-18 who do not have a father figure in their lives, with leadership skills, guidance, godly values, and a continual relationship with mentors. Through teamwork with family, teachers, and counselors, Team Focus offers support in a relaxed, cost-free atmosphere. Visit: Teamfocususa.org or call 251-635-1515/toll free: 877-635-0010 for more information.